series

Care for your
Dog

CONTENTS

Collins

Published by William Collins Sons & Co Ltd
London · Glasgow · Sydney · Auckland · Toronto · Johannesburg

© Royal Society for the Prevention of Cruelty to Animals 1980, 1985, 1990

NEW EDITION

First published 1990

9 8 7 6 5 4 3 2 1

This is a fully revised and extended edition
of *Care for Your Dog*, first published in 1980
and reprinted 10 times, with revisions in 1985

Text of the 1980 edition by Tina Hearne; text
revisions and additions for this edition by Anna Sproule

Designed and edited by Templar Publishing Ltd.,
Pippbrook Mill, Dorking, Surrey

Front cover photograph by Sue Streeter

Text photographs by Animal Photography Ltd, John Clegg, Bruce Coleman Ltd,
Colour Library International, Chris Fairclough, Solitaire *(also back cover, top)*,
Sue Streeter *(also back cover, centre)*, Syndication International, The Northern
Picture Library, Diana Wyllie, ZEFA

Illustrations by Robert Morton (with acknowledgements to photographs by
J.P. Volrath)/Bernard Thornton Artists and Terry Riley/David Lewis Artists

A catalogue record for this book is available from the British Library

Printed in Italy by New Interlitho, Milan

ISBN 0 00 412540 1

I Dogs. II Animals.
1. Title main entry.

First things first, animals are fun. Anybody who has ever enjoyed the company of a pet knows well enough just how strong the bond between human and animal can be. Elderly or lonely people often depend on a pet for their only company, and this can be a rewarding relationship for both human and animal. Doctors have proved that animals can be instrumental in the prevention of and recovery from mental or physical disease. Children learn the meaning of loyalty, unselfishness and friendship by growing up with animals.

But the commitment to an animal is a commitment for the whole of that animal's lifetime – anything up to 20 years of total responsibility for its health and well-being. If you are not prepared for the inevitable expense, time, patience and occasional frustration involved, then the RSPCA would much rather that you didn't have a pet.

Armed with the facts, aware of the pitfalls but still confident of your ability to give a pet a good home, the next step is to find where you can get an animal from. Seek the advice of a veterinary surgeon or RSPCA Inspector about reputable local breeders or suppliers. Do consider the possibility of offering a home to an animal from an RSPCA establishment. There are no animals more deserving of loving owners.

As for the care of your pet, you should find in the following pages all you need to know to keep it happy, healthy and rewarding for many years to come.

Responsible ownership means happy pets. Enjoy the experience!

DAVID WILKINS
Chief Veterinary Officer, RSPCA

Introduction

Mongrel or pedigree, dogs make superb companions for anyone who has the time, the home and the affection to give them.

The diversity of dogs is enormous. In height, they range from the gigantic Irish Wolfhound to the tiny Yorkshire Terrier. They include both the massive Newfoundland, weighing as much as a full-grown man, and the Chihuahua which, at 1 kg/2 lb in weight, is the smallest breed of dog in the world. Their coats vary too, from the smooth satin of the Boxer to the silky plumes of the Maltese and the long 'cords' of the Hungarian Komondor. At the other extreme, the warm, smooth-skinned Mexican Hairless Dog is almost completely bald.

Dogs' abilities and temperaments are as varied as their looks. The herd dogs, bred for hard work, seem completely tireless, while a total contrast is presented by the dignified Pekingese, with its rolling gait and love of an easy life. But, though not a natural athlete, the Pekingese has its own brand of strength. Naturally assertive, it can completely dominate members of a gentler – if much bigger – breed, such as the St Bernard.

These huge differences in appearance and personality are, of course, fully shared by the dogs that outnumber all the pedigree canines: the mongrels. Showing characteristics of every and any breed (and sometimes of no known breeds at all), mongrels make pets that are just as delightful as the pedigree breeds. In terms of health, they even score more highly than the pure-breds, since their 'hybrid vigour' guards them from the genetic abnormalities that can result from selective breeding.

The only real drawback with mongrels is the guesswork that, when small, they impose on their owners. It can be very difficult to tell how they will grow up – or, indeed, how much they will grow. One reason why so many adult dogs are unfortunate enough to need new homes is, quite simply, that they grow too much. But, however hard it is to find, there is a home suited somewhere to every dog and a dog suited to every owner. Ensuring a perfect match between the two is the best of all services that dog-owners can do their pets.

Pedigree or mongrel?

PEDIGREE DOGS

Pedigree, or pure-bred dogs, are the most expensive to buy, but it is not usually difficult to find homes for their puppies. Being highly bred may make them more delicate than dogs of mixed ancestry and more likely to inherit defects. The very fact that they are descended from a line of dogs used traditionally for a particular form of work may make some of them unsuitable as pets for the average household.

Dalmatians, for instance, were once carriage dogs. A pair of them would run alongside the horses in the capacity of outriders. Their elegant proportions and attractive, spotted coats mean they are now in demand as pets, but they should only be kept if they can be allowed plenty of exercise.

CROSS-BRED DOGS

Cross-breds are the progeny of two pure-bred parents of different breeds. Cross-breds usually make very good pets. They are cheaper to buy, but of course cost as much to keep as pedigree dogs.

When both parents are known, it is possible to estimate the adult size and type of a cross-bred puppy. Depending on the combination of the parents' characteristics, a cross-bred dog can be very attractive, and may be stronger in constitution and often less highly strung than either of its parents.

MONGREL DOGS

Mongrels are dogs of mixed ancestry. They are inexpensive and most make affectionate companions. Nearly all mongrels are robust, but since their sires are often unknown, it is impossible to predict accurately how mongrel puppies will develop.

This is one reason why mongrels are difficult to home, and why so many are taken to animal welfare societies, such as the RSPCA, from which they can sometimes be adopted.

Pedigree Irish Setter

Pekingese/Yorkshire Terrier Cross

Mongrel

Neutering

MALE OR FEMALE?

Another question of choice is whether to have a dog o bitch: when unneutered their natures are very different.

The dogs are rather independent. This trait means tha they are more difficult to train and control than bitches. also means that they like to wander off on their own particularly in search of bitches on heat. Those which fin bitches in season will mate them; those frustrated will mak a pathetic attempt to impregnate the family cat or a favour ite cushion. Frustrated dogs tend to be aggressive wit people and other animals. This leads to fighting betwee dogs and to sheep worrying (p.43).

Castration, sedation, and hormonal medication ar means of controlling the ardent nature of the dog.

Bitches are more popular as family pets, and may cost little more. They are usually affectionate and companion able, but unless they are spayed or treated with hormon injections or pills, they will need to be contained securel when on heat. The bitch normally comes into season twic a year, for three weeks at a time. She will nee a really safe enclosure, roofed in, o fenced to a height of 2 m/6 ft. Alter natively, she can be kept indoors, o even sent to a boarding kennel fo these periods.

In short-haired dogs such as these Dalmatians, the external sexual characteristics are clearly visible.

Dog

Bitch

NEUTERING

Unless an owner has definite plans t breed from a dog, the RSPCA strongly recommends that all dogs kept as househol pets should be neutered. At the moment about a million puppies are born every yea in Britain alone. Of these, perhaps over half ar unwanted and, sadly, may have to be destroyed. Neuter ing all dogs not needed for breeding is the single most im portant step that can be taken towards halting this tragi process of destruction.

Isn't it unkind to neuter a healthy dog?

No. For unneutered dogs living in a domestic environment, the sexual urge brings havoc in its wake. As they roam after bitches in season, they have accidents and get into fights. If frustrated, they can become noisy and aggressive.

What about the bitch?

A fertile bitch can bear two litters a year if – as very often happens – she escapes while in season. Constant whelping weakens her health, in addition to increasing the unwanted canine population. Contrary to popular belief, it is not really necessary to allow a bitch to have a litter before being neutered.

What does neutering consist of?

Dogs are usually neutered by castration, or the surgical removal of the testes. Bitches are spayed: this means having their ovaries and uterus (womb) removed. Both operations are done by a veterinary surgeon under a general anaesthetic, and recovery is rapid.

Are there adverse after-effects, such as weight gain or a change in character?

Some dogs can be prone to gain weight, but this is more likely to be due to over-eating than as a direct result of spaying or castration. Neutered animals often need less food than before, and your veterinary surgeon can advise you about adjustments to a dog's diet.

Spaying makes very little difference to the character of a bitch, but the changes in a dog are only for the better: he will no longer suffer from sexual frustration and will be less inclined to roam.

Can neutering be performed at any age?

Ideally, bitches should be spayed before their first season and dogs between seven and twelve months, but dogs of both sexes can be neutered at any age as long as they are fit and healthy. Your veterinary surgeon will advise.

Neutering is in both the dog's interest and the owner's, and neutering your pet will help prevent untold canine suffering. Veterinary surgeons will be happy to answer further questions, and many co-operate with the RSPCA in offering reduced operating fees for low-income owners.

Choosing a dog

Given the time, living space, finances and understanding at an owner's disposal, what sort of dog will be happiest in the home he or she can offer?

MATCHING BREEDS TO HOMES

In general, the extremes of the canine spectrum cannot often be recommended as pets. The giant breeds such as the Great Dane, the St Bernard, and the Irish Wolfhound are kept most satisfactorily in houses with extensive grounds where the dogs can spend plenty of time out of doors. At the other end of the scale, the toy breeds may be too small and delicate for family pets, although they make fine companions for smaller households. Many large breeds like Afghans, German Shepherd Dogs and Old English Sheep dogs can be be remarkbably tolerant of children, and they are good guards as well. But they also need plenty of space. As a general rule, the dogs which are most suited to the rough and tumble of ordinary family life are members of the small to middle-size breeds, such as Terriers, Retrievers and Spaniels.

ADOPTING AN ADULT DOG

Rather than buying or acquiring a puppy, some owners may wish to offer a home to an adult dog – perhaps from an animal sanctuary. Adopting a dog in this way can be even more rewarding than bringing one up from puppyhood but it is also a challenge. To minimize future difficulties, an owner-to-be should find out as much of the dog's past history as possible, and especially why it now needs a new home.

SOURCES

Pedigree puppies are best bought from breeders specializing in the breed required. Names and addresses can be obtained from the relevant breed club, or via the Kennel Club. A good rule is always to see the puppy with its mother. In all cases, buyers should avoid pet shops and

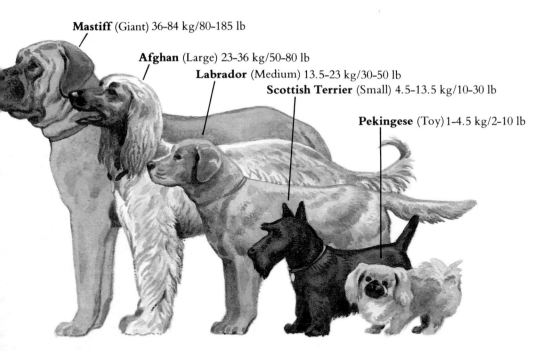

Mastiff (Giant) 36–84 kg/80–185 lb

Afghan (Large) 23–36 kg/50–80 lb

Labrador (Medium) 13.5–23 kg/30–50 lb

Scottish Terrier (Small) 4.5–13.5 kg/10–30 lb

Pekingese (Toy) 1–4.5 kg/2–10 lb

Both the Mastiff on the left and the Peke on the right need a very special kind of owner. Dogs like the Labrador in the centre make the best pets for ordinary family life.

'puppy supermarkets'. Adults can be acquired from breed rescue associations. Mongrels can be obtained from a wider variety of sources, such as family friends or animal sanctuaries.

SIGNS OF HEALTH

When choosing a dog of any type, the owner-to-be should carefully check its health, both physical and mental. A healthy dog has bright, clear eyes and a dense coat without scabs or bald patches. A dog with signs of diarrhoea should be avoided. Buyers should also note a dog's reaction to their presence. Timid, cringing dogs or puppies should not be chosen, even out of pity. Nor should dogs that seem over-assertive, let alone aggressive.

All buyers should have the dog's health checked by a veterinary surgeon as soon as possible. They should also reserve the right to return the dog to where it was obtained if the result is unsatisfactory.

Every dog should have been vaccinated regularly against the major canine diseases (p.35) and have an up-to-date certificate recording initial vaccination and subsequent boosters. The veterinary surgeon will advise on when the next boosters are due. A dog with no certificate should be vaccinated as soon as possible.

Breed types

Dog breeders everywhere divide the pedigree dog breeds into separate groups, according to the history of the breeds involved. The groups and their names differ slightly from country to country, but, in general, there are six: hounds, terriers, gundogs, working dogs, utility dogs and toys.

As their name implies, toy dogs are always small. So, with one or two exceptions, are terriers. Dogs in the other groups vary in size, with working dogs ranging from the low-slung Welsh Corgi to the towering Great Dane.

Recognizable traits such as size, shape, and coat texture and colour can also, of course, be inherited by cross-bred dogs and mongrels.

HOUNDS
Hounds were all originally bred to hunt other animals by either sight or scent. Members of the sight-hunting group include the Irish Wolfhound, the Borzoi (also bred to hunt wolves), the Greyhound and Saluki (both bred to hunt members of the deer family), and the Afghan and the Rhodesian Ridgeback, bred to hunt leopards and lions respectively. All are long-legged and swift.

Some of the scent hounds, like the Bloodhound, are also tall, long-legged dogs. But others, such as the Basset, are short-legged or otherwise compactly built. All scent hounds have the built-in urge and stamina to roam over the countryside in pursuit of a scent.

WORKING DOGS
These are the dogs that were first bred for herding, guarding, pulling carts or sleighs, or – in the case of the St Bernard and the Newfoundland – rescue work in snow or water. The breeds trained to herd sheep and cattle include the Collie, German Shepherd Dog, Old English Sheepdog, and Welsh Corgi. The Komondor and the Pyrenean Mountain Dog were bred to guard flocks against predators. Other guard breeds include the Boxer, Bull Mastiff, Great Dane and Dobermann Pinscher. Two arctic breeds, the

German Shepherd Dog

Dobermann Pinschers

at-coated Retriever

nglish Setter

hasa Apso

Alaskan Malamute and the Siberian Husky, are famous for their sledge-pulling work. All working breeds are country dogs, and must have plenty of room for exercise.

GUNDOGS
These breeds were created to help in the sport of shooting game birds and waterfowl. They are trained to find game or to retrieve it, both on land and in the water. Bred to co-operate rather than to kill, they are obedient and dependable. Gundogs include Setters, Pointers, Spaniels and Retrievers. The good-natured Labrador and Golden Retrievers both fall into this group.

TERRIERS
These are the smallest of the hunting breeds. Their name comes from the Latin word for earth, *terra*. As it implies, they were bred to hunt animals that live in underground burrows. The names of individual breeds – from Airedale to West Highland – often carry a reminder of the big country estates where they were first created. Terriers are lively, loyal, tough, fearless, and extremely energetic. They can be aggressive with strangers – and digging is in their nature!

UTILITY DOGS
Utility dogs (in some countries called 'Non-sporting dogs') are breeds which do not fall into the hunting or working groups, but which were once bred to a particular role (shown here in brackets). They include the Bulldog (bull-baiting), Chow Chow (bred in China for its fur and meat), the Keeshond (guard dog on Dutch barges), and Dalmatian (escorting carriages).

TOY DOGS
Bred purely as pets or for the show bench, these are often miniature versions of the large breeds. Popular toy breeds include the Chihuahua, King Charles Spaniel, Italian Greyhound, Maltese, Papillon, Pekingese, Pomeranian, Pug, and Yorkshire Terrier. Toy dogs are inexpensive to feed and need little exercise but, owing to selective breeding, they tend to be delicate and rather excitable.

The toy breeds are not alone in suffering from the effects of inbreeding, so veterinary examination before acquisition (see p.9) is recommended.

Biology

Tail The dog's natural tail serves a variety of biological uses. It protects the vulnerable hind parts, acts as a balance when running, acts as a rudder when swimming, and is the most obvious means of communication.

Traditionally, however, certain breeds of dog have had part of the tail amputated, or docked, to leave stumps of varying length. Breeds well-known for their lack of tail include the Pembroke Welsh Corgi and the Old English Sheepdog (indeed, the latter's alternative name is 'Bobtail'), but the standards for other, often similar, breeds have not called for docking. Practice of this mutilation has been therefore very much an arbitrary one, and today docking a dog for cosmetic purposes is increasingly frowned on.

The RSPCA has campaigned against the practice of tail docking for many years and many countries ban docking outright.

Backbone Because the backbone is less well supported in the long-backed, short-legged dogs such as the Dachshund, these breeds are the most susceptible to spinal disc problems. Symptoms include pain and weakness in the hindquarters, or actual paralysis. The symptoms can occur suddenly and often after a violent movement such as a fall or a jump. The risk of such injury is increased if the backbone has to bear the extra strain imposed by obesity. Veterinary treatment, together with good nursing, is likely to effect at least partial recovery.

Feet Long-haired dogs, and those with feathered feet, tend to collect grass seeds and grit which puncture the skin and enter the foot, causing pain and interdigital cysts. Long hair on the feet can also cover the claws and prevent their being worn down naturally by friction. This can cause the claws to become ingrown. It is therefore advisable to clip long hair between the toes, especially in summer.

Deposits of tar, salt, detergents, oil, cement dust, etc., on road or floor surfaces may cause interdigital eczema. Clean such irritant substances off pads with soap and water; take veterinary advice if the pads are badly contaminated.

Claws The claws grow throughout life, and may need cutting from time to time. Neglected claws can grow in a circle and penetrate the foot to cause great pain and lameness. The dew claws are especially liable to become overgrown in this way, and the veterinary surgeon may advise removal.

Ears By nature dogs have erect ears, like the German Shepherd Dog, and breeds which retain them suffer fewer problems as a result. Because of poor air circulation, dogs with folded ears are more prone to bacterial infection of the outer ear canal than those with erect ears. Those with woolly coats that do not moult – Poodles, Bedlington Terriers, Old English Sheepdogs – need the hair in the ear regularly plucked to improve air circulation, and to allow flakes of dried wax to escape normally. Wax can also be trapped by the heavy ears of Spaniels, which also

Paw showing dew claw

Ears of German Shepherd Dog

tend to pick up grass seeds in summer that can cause them very great discomfort.

Eyes Certain breeds, such as the Boston Terrier, have been bred with protuberant eyes. They are more liable to eye injury than breeds with normal eyes, and need to excrete excessive tear fluid, for cleaning and lubrication, that tends to run down the face, since the orb of the eye distorts the tear duct and prevents proper drainage into the nose.

Breeds such as the Bulldog may have watery eyes if the lower lids are stretched down by the presence of excessive skin. Other breeds, e.g. Chow and Spaniels, may have watery eyes and intense irritation if the lids turn in to cause the eyelashes to brush across the eyes. Abnormalities such as ingrowing eyelashes and a second row of eyelashes need veterinary attention.

Golden Retriever

Teeth The dog, being a natural carnivore, has teeth well adapted to puncture, tear and slice flesh, and to grind bones. The most noticeable teeth are the fangs. These are so prominent in dogs that they are known in all beasts as the canines, a word derived from the Latin *Canis*, a dog. The particular function of the canines is that of a weapon. The dog uses them to hold its prey, and to puncture and tear at the flesh. In all the dog has 42 teeth, whereas the cat has only 30. This can lead to serious overcrowding in short-nosed breeds such as the Pug, with resultant malocclusion and premature loss.

Gnawing on a bone, hard biscuit or dog chew does exercise the jaws, helps to clean the teeth, and gives the dog pleasure, but it will not prevent the formation of tartar on the inside of the teeth. Tartar formation depends on the alkalinity or acidity of the saliva. A deposit of tartar predisposes the dog to caries, pyorrhoea and exposed tooth roots. Most dogs will need their teeth scaled by a veterinary surgeon from time to time after the age of about six years. Toy breeds are more likely to need their teeth scaled at an earlier age.

Head The head-shape varies enormously, from the very long-nosed Greyhound to the short-nosed Bulldog. These extremes of shape, which are the result of selective breeding, have endowed the breeds with very short heads with a number of disadvantages.

The teeth of short-nosed dogs are overcrowded and tend to fall out prematurely. In breeds like the Shar Pei, with its deeply-furrowed skin, eczema or an abscess may develop in the facial skin folds. Breeds with short, broad heads, like the Boston Terrier, have difficulty in giving birth. In some breeds, the shortened head has led to the development of a large soft palate hanging over the trachea. These breeds have difficulty in breathing, and are at risk under an anaesthetic.

Short-nosed Bulldog

Long-nosed Greyhound

The short-nosed Pug

Bedding

Although many working dogs and gundogs are kept in outdoor kennels, the majority of pet dogs probably live in their owners' homes. Their only accommodation is their own bed, and this is very important to them. The bed is the dog's own territory: the place where it keeps its valuables, and the only part of the house where it can be sure other members of the family will not intrude.

For a puppy, the ideal bed is a cardboard box, with a 'gateway' cut in one side. As the puppy outgrows its bed (or chews it up), it can be replaced with another, bigger one. Adult dogs, though, need something more permanent.

Rigid plastic bed Washable, light, draughtproof, waterproof, inexpensive, reasonably resistant to chewing.

TYPES OF BED AND BEDDING
Dog beds are available in a wide variety of designs and sizes, from Toy to Giant. One type is the expensive but useful Battersea bed, which is made of moulded fibreglass with a metal edge, and is used in RSPCA kennels. Another very popular one is the rigid plastic bed. Some dogs delight in chewing the corners off the plastic bed's gateway, but it is much sturdier in this respect than the traditional wicker basket. Lined with a washable cushion, however, a basket makes a good bed for a non-chewing dog.

Home-made bed Adequate if right size for dog, draughtproof, comfortable, dry and easily cleaned or replaced.

A newer type of bed is the large, squashy 'bean bag'. The bean bag is attractive, comfortable, extremely portable, and will fit easily into a corner: something that dogs enjoy.

Whichever type of bed is chosen, it should be big enough to allow the dog to go through its primordial routine of turning round and round before settling to sleep. In all cases except the bean bag, the bed should be lined with newspaper, topped by comfortable bedding such as a cushion, a towel, or an old blanket.

Folding travel bed Also available: 'beanbags', and moulded foam beds: neither suitable for dogs that chew.

POSITIONING THE BED
Dogs like a quiet place to sleep in, but they also like to feel part of the family group. A dog's bed should be positioned

somewhere that meets both these requirements, such as a quiet corner of the living room. The spot chosen should be free from draughts, and away from the main passage of feet.

Dogs should not be allowed to sleep on the household's beds or other items of furniture, however much they may try to. One reasons is that some dense-coated breeds, such as the German Shepherd Dog, tend to have greasy fur that quickly soils soft furnishings. Another is the difficulty an owner will face if the dog picks up fleas. As explained on pp.36–7, these can only be controlled if the dog's bed and bedding are also kept free from infestation.

CLEANING AND HYGIENE
All bedding should be aired daily, and washed or replaced at least once a week. Plastic beds can be washed out, but must be carefully dried out before being used again.

Outdoor kennels need regular attention, too. Four or five times a year, they should be washed out and disinfected. Kennel runs should be hosed down daily, and faeces removed. Faeces left in the garden should also be removed daily.

ith one paw lolling
mfortably, a Cocker Spaniel
kes its ease in a traditional
icker basket, lined with a soft,
arm blanket.

Housing

Privacy Dogs should not be left alone all day, but all dogs need some privacy away from the family if they are to maintain a quiet, well-balanced disposition. When denied a place of their own and time to be alone, dogs tend to grow neurotic and demanding, resorting to abnormal behavioural traits such as self-mutilation, and howling or barking constantly when, inevitably, they have to be left alone for a period.

In the house it is difficult to find a place for the dog's bed that will never be disturbed by the family; in the garden all dogs can be given their own kennel whether or not they will sleep out at night. A good kennel can be of great benefit to all dogs during the day: a place of their own where they can rest in comfort and security.

Two quite distinct types of kennel are illustrated here. One has a small run incorporated into the design; the other is the traditional design best sited within a safely fenced garden or within an enclosure.

The garden A safely enclosed garden, or part of one, should be thought of as a necessity for all dogs. If their own garden is well fenced, with secure gates, the dogs will be able to enjoy hours of freedom denied to those which are shut indoors between walks.

Dogs need to be let out into the garden early in the morning to urinate, and then several more times a day, to urinate again and to defecate. This is where dogs should defecate. It takes only moments to remove the faeces daily.

Traditional garden kennel The interior of any dog kennel needs to be roomy enough for the dog to be able to stand up, lie down and turn around with ease. If appropriately sized, the traditional type of kennel is very suitable. The roof should be pitched to shed rain and snow, and to give extra headroom.

Extended eaves ensure that rain does not drive or splash up into the kennel entrance. To facilitate cleaning, the front opens like two doors, while the floor is lifted 10 cm/4 in off the ground to avoid rising damp. The entrance is sited at the front rather than at the gable end, where the bed would

Running chain

main wire
attached
to kennel

swivel

lead chain –
long enough
for dog to
enter kennel

swivel

be in a direct draught. Draughts can also be prevented by the installation over the entrance of a dog-flap. The sleeping compartment should always be furthest from the entrance.

The kennel's exterior is most usually clad with tongued and grooved timber over a timber frame, with lining boards fitted to the interior for extra insulation. If the pitched roof is hinged, it can be propped open for extra ventilation in very hot weather. The kennel should be positioned in a dry, sheltered place. It should face away from the prevailing wind, and away from the midday sun in summer.

Kennel incorporating
run One type of kennel widely available incorporates a small run. Because there is plenty of

headroom, this design is suitable for the larger, taller breeds, and for bitches on heat, which can be safely contained within the high walls of the run.

Easy access to the kennel interior, for cleaning or for attending a sick dog, must be considered in advance and built into the design. In the kennel illustrated such access is easy.

Not all large dogs are comfortable using a dog bed. In this design of kennel the bed is a low platform, raised off the kennel floor and made comfortable with bedding materials such as washable rugs, cushions and blankets arranged on a layer of straw, wood-wool, or strips of torn paper. Squashy 'bean bags' and moulded foam beds can be very warm and comfortable in these conditions.

The running chain No dog should be chained permanently, nor even for long periods. Chained dogs become both physically and mentally frustrated. They suffer boredom as a result of lack of companionship, and exasperation as a result of enforced physical restraint. They may also suffer physical hardship as a result of lack of warmth, shade, water, and so on. In extreme cases they will chafe or damage the neck by constantly tugging at the collar.

However, if a dog has to be tethered for a short period, the running chain can be recommended (always providing it is used with care).

As shown above, a taut line of gauge 8 wire, fitted with a swivel, is fixed between the kennel and a convenient upright. A light chain is attached to the swivel which, when necessary, can be clipped to the dog's collar. The line should always be placed so that the dog can enter its kennel. When the taut line is attached to a post, there will need to be a stop on the line, made from a bulldog clamp (from ironmongers' stores), positioned to prevent the running chain reaching right up to the post. If the stop is not used, the dog will entangle its chain tightly round the post.

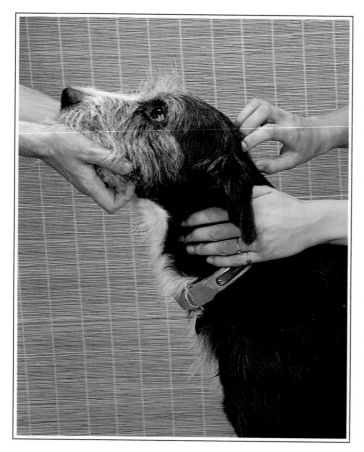

Creating the bond of friendship. As both his new owners fondle him, this Irish Wolfhound makes the all-important eye contact. Trust established now will form the foundation of a relationship that will last for the dog's lifetime.

Introducing the new dog

The day a dog is introduced to its new home is one of the most important of its life. Even for an adult dog, the change can be confusing. For a puppy, which has known nothing but the familiar comfort of its dam and siblings, the new surroundings are bewildering and even frightening.

The best way to calm the newcomer's fears is to ensure that the introduction takes place as smoothly as possible. Before the dog arrives, the owner should have decided where it will sleep, where its food and water bowls should go, and which parts of the house it should be allowed access

Introductions are often easiest when pets are young. But this pair should not be left alone together until the cat has got used to its big companion.

As shown here, children can become expert at handling pets. This farmer's boy and farmer's dog probably grew up together.

o. The garden should be made escape-proof. On the day tself, the bed and bowls should be put out, and the dog's ollar, identity tag and lead must also be ready for their wearer.

CHILDREN AND OTHER PETS

When the dog arrives, let it explore its new territory as it wishes. This will give it confidence, and will also give the owner a chance to observe it. Appropriate action can then be taken over any obvious habits or fears. Warn children that it needs time to settle down, and that it will be alarmed by sudden noises and movements. Do not leave very young children unsupervised with a dog. Introductions to other pets should be handled carefully and gradually. Again, supervision is important. Take care to make a special fuss of the older pets, so as to reassure them that the newcomer has not robbed them of their place in the household.

Feeding

Although dogs are classed as carnivores, they do not need an all-meat diet. But they do need a well-balanced one. This means feeding them enough high-quality protein, fat and carbohydrates to meet their daily nutritional requirements. The actual choice is up to the owner – and the dog.

Dogs react differently to different foods, and one dog's favourite meal may be another's poison. It is even possible to find dogs with whom meat itself disagrees. In this case, the answer is to give one of the non-meat dog foods that are now available. Vegetarians and vegans may wish to do the same for their dogs, but all non-meat dog foods should be used only with veterinary advice.

Feeding times   Some large breeds are content with only one meal a day, usually fed in the evening. These dogs have a big enough stomach to take a day's food at one time, and do not need to worry and scavenge for titbits between mealtimes. However, some very large breeds (such as the Great Dane or Irish Wolfhound) require so much that they need to have their daily food intake split into two. They are fed half their rations in the morning, and half in the evening. The same routine is needed for small dogs and old dogs.

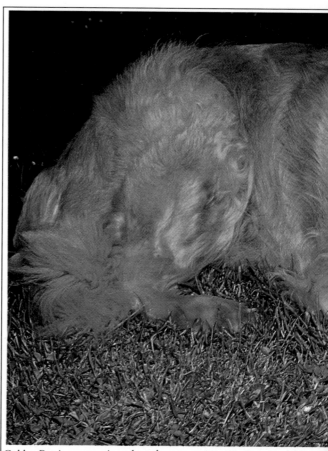

Golden Retriever gnawing a large bone

Other dogs can also be fed twice a day, but with the main meat meal reserved for the evening. The morning meal is made up of biscuit or cereal, perhaps given with milk.

Once an owner has decided when to feed a dog, the feeding timetable should be kept to regularly. It is better to feed after exercise rather than before it. If a dog has a morning meal, feed it after its walk rather than before. This is particularly important in warm weather.

Fresh food   Meat is the staple food of dogs. Probably the most economical way to provide meat is to buy minced beef and inexpensive cuts, such as ox cheek, together with cheap liver and other offal. High-quality fresh meat may be fed raw. Other meat and all offal should be cooked before use. (Offal should not be fed too often, since it can cause diarrhoea.) Fed with biscuit that has added vitamins and minerals, a varied diet of this sort supplies all nutrients.

Convenience foods   There is a wide range of packeted, frozen and canned convenience foods now available. Follow the manufacturer's feeding instructions. Some convenience foods are all meat, needing the addition of biscuit or cereal. Others are 'all-in-one' dried foods, which need no added carbohydrate content. These can be especially useful if, for any reason, a dog has trouble digesting meat. They can increase a dog's thirst so, if they are used, plenty of water *must* always be available.

Biscuit and cereal   The main source of carbohydrate in a dog's diet is dog biscuit or dog meal, often obtainable with added vitamins and minerals. It can be fed mixed with meat, or on its own. Large dog biscuits make goo[d] between-meals treats, and exercise a dog's jaws. Dogs al[so] enjoy cereals such as cooked rice or porridge. Cooked ri[ce] can be better than dog biscuit for a dog with diarrhoea.

Bones All dogs appreciate a bone. But they should *nev[er]* be given small bones that splinter, such as those from lam[b], chicken, or any type of chop. Cooked bones must also [be] avoided. However, a large raw marrow bone cleans a dog[s] teeth, massages its gums, and becomes a valued possessio[n]. Bones of this type are particularly good for dogs fed on so[ft] food. All dogs also enjoy rawhide chews.

Vegetables In the wild, dogs eat some vegetable matt[er] directly. They also take in some indirectly, when they e[at] the stomach contents of their herbivorous prey. Pet do[gs] can have some cooked vegetables included in their die[t], mainly for roughage. Carrots are often a favourite, an[d] cooked potatoes can also be given. Dogs also like to che[w] grass. If they have eaten something that disagrees wit[h] them, the grass will help make them vomit.

Drinking water Fresh drinking water must always b[e] available. This is particularly important if a dog is fed on a[n] 'all-in-one' dried food.

Milk Milk is a useful dietary supplement for pregna[nt] and nursing bitches, for puppies, and any dog needing ext[ra] nourishment.

Fresh meat: feed an equal *weight* of cereal food
Canned meat: feed an equal *volume* of cereal food

Food requirements for adult dogs

Type of Breed		Meat (weight when raw)	Canned food 400g/14oz cans
Toy:	up to 4.5 kg (10 lb)	85–110 g (3–4 oz)	⅓–½
Small:	4.5–13.5 kg (10–30 lb)	up to 225 g (8 oz)	½–1
Medium:	13.5 kg–23 kg (30–50 lb)	about 335 g (12 oz)	1–1½
Large:	23–36 kg (50–80 lb)	about 560 g (20 oz)	1½–2
Giant:	over 36 kg (80 lb)	560–900 g (20–32 oz)	2–3

The Beagle, a small hound bred to hunt by scent

The Afghan Hound was bre

The Cairn is a bold and lively terrier

The Welsh Springer Spaniel, a reliable gun dog

The Golden Retriever, a gun dog bred to retrieve dead birds

embroke Corgi was bred as a working dog

The Yorkshire Terrier, a popular toy dog

Exercise

As a species, dogs are strongly built, with a large lung capacity, giving them both speed and stamina. The actual amount of exercise needed by the different breeds varies greatly, but is usually in proportion to their size.

All dogs, whether they need a lot of exercise or a little, need to be exercised regularly – at least once a day, and possibly twice. The energetic breeds, in particular, are capable of taking a considerable amount of daily walking and running. They quickly become bored, restless and unhappy if denied the physical effort and mental stimulus this gives them. The big mongrels, the hounds, gundogs, working dogs, some of the utility breeds, and terriers such as the Airedale, Border, Fox and Lakeland, are built and bred for sustained physical output. The fittest of them will enjoy as much as 16 km/10 miles a day.

One of the exceptions is the Bulldog. It was bred as a fighting dog, and its massive build, with all the power concentrated in the shoulders, is unsuitable for running.

Ideally dogs need to be taken where they can safely be let off the lead to run free, with no risk from traffic, and no threat to farm livestock or wildlife. All their exercise, even that taken off the lead, should be supervised and the dogs kept within calling distance.

Unsupervised, dogs will rove freely over the country-side, and will certainly search out bitches on heat and lay siege to their homes. The Labrador Retriever, in particular, has the reputation of being an inveterate rover. Indeed, many mongrels show signs of having been sired by a Labrador.

The smallest breeds can manage with very little exercise. A distance of 1.5 km/1 mile is enough, and this is likely to be achieved by running free in their own garden. They do, however, appreciate a change of scene, even if they are too small, too slow, or too delicate to be taken far.

Short-nosed and toy breeds may be more comfortably exercised in a harness rather than the more usual collar and lead. Check chains – which, wrongly fastened, can live up

'Halti' headcollar

Check chain: right way

Check chain: wrong way

to the more common name of choke chain – can be used for training big, boisterous dogs. The check chain should be looped so that the slipping ring, by its weight, loosens the collar immediately the dog stops pulling (see left). Improperly used, the check chain can inflict serious injury. A safe alternative is the bridle-like 'Halti' headcollar (left). This gives a dog freedom to open its mouth, but closes the jaws shut if the dog pulls on the lead.

Every year farmers lose many thousands of sheep and lambs as a result of dog worrying. Either the livestock are victims of direct attacks by dogs, or they are stillborn after dogs have chased pregnant ewes.

When in the vicinity of livestock, it is always advisable – and often a legal requirement – to keep dogs on the lead.

In certain circumstances, a farmer may legally shoot a dog for worrying livestock (p.42).

Dogs really cannot be expected to negotiate roads safely by themselves, and in a growing number of towns it is an offence to allow an unleashed dog on the streets (p.42). One of the main reasons is that they are a hazard to traffic.

When crossing a road with a dog, the same procedure has to be followed, regardless of traffic conditions. It should be a matter of habit to halt at the kerb, and the dog must always sit until told to cross.

Dogs need to be taken to an open space every day, for interest and for exercise. In towns and cities the only space available, within walking distance, may be the local park, which is one reason why certain energetic breeds of dog are totally unsuitable for urban life.

Since parks are also children's playgrounds and leisure areas for the whole population, owners should always clear up their pets' faeces, which can constitute a health hazard. Many leisure parks have restrictions on exercising dogs, but they remain a great boon to the urban dog owner.

Training

All dogs need some basic training if they are to have good relationships with their owners. An untrained dog is a liability to itself and its household, and a danger to other people. To behave in public, a dog needs to understand three basic orders: 'Come', 'Sit' and 'Stay'. Dogs also need to learn how to walk on a lead and, for this, the command 'Heel' is very useful.

Whatever the age, rewards and approval have a much greater effect than punishment, and training sessions should be made as pleasant as possible for the 'pupil'. Reproofs should be minimal, and must immediately follow the offence. Otherwise, the dog will not understand what it has done wrong.

Training should start in puppyhood, with the main techniques being patience and 'little and often'. It is quite possible to re-train dogs that have become set in their ways, but the patience needed is even greater. Inexperienced owners can learn effective training techniques at a dog-training class. Details of local classes are often displayed in veterinary surgeons' premises.

To teach a dog to 'Come', call its name, followed by the word 'Come!' Pat the front of your legs; dogs respond to gestures as well as to words. Make a great fuss of it when it arrives. Repeat as often as possible. If training outdoors in an area where dogs must be kept on leads, use a long training lead.

To teach 'Sit', put the dog on its lead. Holding the lead in the right hand, position the dog on your left. Say 'Sit!' and press the dog's hindquarters down with your left hand. Keep its head up with the lead. When it is sitting, make a fuss of it. Repeat frequently, both on and off the lead.

Use a long training lead to teach 'Stay'. Make the dog sit, and stand in front of it. Raise one hand, flat palm outwards, and say 'Stay!' Move slowly backwards a few steps, repeating the command. Praise the dog if it stays still. If the dog moves, scold it and make it sit down again, then re-start the exercise. Repeat frequently, lengthening the distance you move backwards.

Boarding and travelling

Sooner or later, most owners need to find a boarding kennel where their dog can stay while they are away on holiday. Boarding accommodation needs to be booked well in advance, if possible at the same time as the family's holiday is arranged. No reputable kennel will accept a dog without vaccination papers. Details of the dog's medical history should also be given.

The great majority of dogs quicky adapt to life in a kennel, although a few may pine badly. To choose a kennel where a dog will have every chance of being happy, some prior research is necessary. Kennels in the area should be visited, and their accommodation inspected.

The number of staff should be noted, as should their attitude. Sympathetic staff and a high staff ratio mean dogs will have a good chance of individual attention. The kennel's local authority licence to operate should be on display, or available for inspection.

Dogs are exercised individually at this RSPCA kennels.

Security The kennel accommmodation chosen must be safe, and the staff must be security conscious. A door need be opened only for a few seconds for a dog to escape.

Hygiene It is very important to choose a kennel that is clean and hygienic, and not smelly. Faeces should not be lying around, and feeding dishes and water bowls should always be clean. The kitchen where the animals' food is prepared should be especially clean and well-organized.

Accommodation The dogs' houses should be dry, clean and roomy, with heating for use as necessary. The attached outdoor run should be roofed in, with an escape-proof concrete floor.

Exercise Different facilities are on offer. It is for the owner to decide between a communal run (offering freedom but also the risk of cross-infection), and kennels that walk their dogs individually in their own paddock.

Dogs in cars

Most dogs enjoy an outing in a car, particularly in a car familiar to them. It is wise to accustom them to car travel while they are young. The space inside the tailgate of a hatchback car is ideal for a dog passenger, but many dogs seem to feel more secure on the car's back seat. On no account should dogs be shut into a car boot.

Dogs which do not travel well, suffering anxiety and perhaps car sickness, may need tranquillizing for an unavoidable journey. Veterinary advice is needed on whether to give sedative or an anti-motion sickness drug. Many dogs, however, do in the end grow out of car sickness.

To encourage the dog settle down for a long trip, it helps to take its own rug or cushion. The car should be well ventilated, and the driver should take frequent short breaks. During these, the dog can have a few minutes' exercise on the lead, and a chance to urinate. Drivers should also carry drinking water for their passenger (plus a bowl), especially in warm weather. Dogs have a low heat tolerance and, on any day when people are feeling uncomfortably hot, a dog will be feeling more uncomfortable still.

Dogs left in cars can be in great danger, even when an open window gives ventilation. Dogs should *never* be left in a motor vehicle – even if parked in the shade – when the weather is sunny (whether hot or cold outside), or likely to become so. The same applies to leaving dogs in caravans, tents, and boats. Dogs left in these conditions can die within a few hours, and their owners can be prosecuted. If members of the public see a dog which seems to be in distress in an unattended vehicle, they should notify the police or the RSPCA at once.

People who regularly have to transport their dogs by car are likely to have chosen an estate model. The dogs can then have their own compartment at the rear, behind a dog guard.

Grooming

BRUSHING AND COMBING

Grooming is good for all dogs, although some need far more than others. Grooming removes dust, dead skin, loose hairs, burrs and tangles. It also massages the skin and improves the tone of the underlying muscles. Parasites are exposed, and the owner can examine the dog for the signs of health listed on p.35.

The accessories used depend on the coat type. Medium and long-haired dogs need a nylon or natural bristle brush, and a metal comb. A very stiff brush is needed for wire-haired breeds. For all the longer-haired breeds, a curry comb is useful for removing hair while the dog is moulting.

Short-haired dogs can be groomed with a mitt called a hound glove. This has short wire bristles on one side, and a ribbed fabric covering on the other.

Daily grooming is recommended, although it may be very brief for some dogs. The long-haired breeds are the ones that must become accustomed to accept grooming as part of their daily routine. Long and medium-length coats need to be brushed first (always with the nap of the coat), then combed. Tangles should be gently teased out or carefully removed with scissors. Dogs with short coats should first be groomed with the bristle side of the mitt. Then they should be stroked hard, or 'polished', with the fabric side.

BATHING

There should be no hesitation about bathing a dog which is dirty or smelling, although it is generally thought only two or three baths are needed in a year. Too frequent bathing will result in the coat becoming dry and brittle as the natural oils are lost.

Apply a proprietary dog shampoo twice during the session, thoroughly rinsing off each application. After-wards it is important to dry the dog as quickly as possible, either with a towel or using a hairdryer. It will also be necessary to groom the dog.

Grooming kit

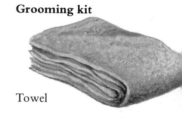

Towel

Mitt for
short-haired dogs

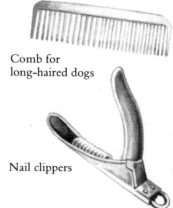

Brush for medium and
long-haired dogs

Comb for
long-haired dogs

Nail clippers

CLIPPING CLAWS

Certain light-footed dogs, like Poodles, may fail to wear down their claws naturally. It is best to have the claws clipped professionally first time, so that the dog can be approached with confidence if it is subsequently necessary to do the clipping oneself. Use animal nail clippers, and avoid cutting into the blood and nerve supply at the base of the nail.

Coat types

Long-haired: Rough Collies

Long   The long-haired coats are attractive, but the most difficult to manage, needing constant attention if they are to remain well groomed. Long-haired dogs can suffer impaired vision because hair falls over the eyes; also they tend to pick up grass seeds in summer unless their feet are clipped. Many cross-breds and mongrels have long hair, and long-haired breeds include the Afghan, Chow Chow, Maltese, Old English Sheepdog, Rough Collie, Samoyed and Yorkshire Terrier.

Medium   The medium-length coats are probably best, and they are certainly easy to care for. These breeds include the Corgis, the Cairn and Border Terriers, the German Shepherd Dog, Labrador Retrievers, Saluki and the Spaniels. These dogs moult a great deal, but need less grooming, and the coat affords them adequate protection from the weather.

Medium-haired: Retriever

Short   Although dogs are generally very hardy, the short-coated breeds are not very well protected from the weather and may need to wear a dog-coat in winter. It is sometimes suggested that they may also be more susceptible to demodectic mange (see p.37). Short-haired breeds include the Basset, Beagle, Boxer, Smooth Dachshund, Greyhound, Pointer, Pug and Whippet.

Wire and wool   The wool coats of the Poodles, the Soft-Coated Wheaten Terrier and the Bedlington Terrier do not moult, but need expert clipping. The wire-coated breeds, including the Airedale, Irish, Lakeland, Norwich, Scottish, Sealyham, Welsh and West Highland White Terriers, Griffon, Irish Wolfhound and Schnauzer need little grooming, but may need expert stripping on occasion during the year.

Wire-haired: Airedale

The healthy dog

Dogs are generally very hardy and healthy. Prevention and a watchful eye are the keys to keeping them that way.

The table opposite shows the signs of a healthy dog. If dogs deviate from these in any way, they need veterinary attention. Do not try home cures, or give human medicine.

Before a dog is prescribed tablets, the veterinary surgeon may want to know its body weight. Most dogs can be weighed at home on the bathroom scales, with the owner holding the dog. The combined weight is noted, then the owner's weight is subtracted from the total.

Veterinary fees can add up, so it makes sense to take out an insurance policy against major veterinary expenses. The RSPCA strongly advises dog owners to take out pet insurance, which should also include cover for any damage their dogs cause.

In perfect health. To this spirited pet, clearing a park bench is no trouble at all.

VACCINATIONS

All dogs should be vaccinated against the infectious canine diseases of distemper, canine hepatitis, leptospirosis, canine parvovirus and kennel cough. The initial protection given by a series of injections in puppyhood does not last for life, however, and protection only continues if adult dogs are given regular booster injections, usually at intervals of one or two years, in accordance with veterinary advice.

Immunity is vital not only for the dog's own health, but to prevent these serious diseases from spreading among the canine population. No boarding kennel should accept a dog without an up-to-date vaccination certificate.

IGNS OF HEALTH

Abdomen	tapering towards hind legs; not distended or unduly sensitive to touch
Anus	clean, with no staining or scouring
Appetite	enthusiastic for food, eating their meals fast; no undue scavenging; no vomiting
Breathing	quiet and even when at rest; panting to cool down; no coughing
Claws	no splits, no overgrown claws; no interdigital cysts
Coat	clean, glossy; free from parasites, loose hairs and dirt
Demeanour	alert, vital; quickly responsive to sounds and calls
Ears	alert to slightest sound; clean, with no deposit; head and ears held at normal angle; no irritation or scratching
Eyes	clear; not unduly sensitive to light; no discharge; not bloodshot
Faeces	vary according to diet, but should be passed regularly: once a day for small dogs; three or four times for large
Movement	good stamina in youth, deteriorating with age: even in age retaining ability to jump small heights, and get into car unaided. Should move with an even gait, with weight evenly distributed on all four legs
Nose	condition depends on environment: likely to be cold and damp on a walk, dry and warm indoors; no persistent discharge
Skin	supple, clean, without scurf, inflammation, parasites or sores
Teeth	clean, without tartar, with strong gums
Urine	passes urine with no difficulty: entire male dogs spray small quantities of urine in house and garden to mark territory

Ailments and parasites

AILMENTS

Like any other animal, humans included, dogs can suffer from a wide variety of ailments, ranging from allergies to rickets. Some of these – such as tumours, arthritis, and heart trouble – are mainly associated with older dogs. Protection against the dangerous canine diseases such as distemper can be given by vaccination. All owners develop a sense of how a dog looks and behaves when in good health. An owner who notices any change in a pet's appearance and behaviour should not attempt home diagnosis. Veterinary help should be promptly sought.

A dog flea

FLEAS

All dogs can sometimes pick up parasites, one of the commonest being fleas. These cause the dog intense irritation, and also act as an intermediate host of tapeworms. They should therefore be eliminated quickly.

A flea infestation should be treated with one of the proprietary preparations available from veterinary surgeons and used according to instructions. As fleas breed in the dog's bedding, it is also important to destroy the eggs they have laid. Do this by burning or washing the bedding and disinfecting any other likely breeding places: measures that are as essential as treating the dog itself. If there are other pets in the household they should be treated too, with similar attention paid to their bedding.

Flea larva is found in bedding

LICE

Unlike fleas, lice spend their entire life-cycle on the dog's body. They multiply very quickly, and a severe infestation causes the dog extreme discomfort, and possibly anaemia. Puppies, in particular, are seriously weakened by them.

Lice cling to the skin, or burrow into it, and are not easily seen, but their white eggs, or nits, can be found in the fur. A dog with a dirty, patchy coat may well be infected with lice and should be taken for veterinary examination without delay.

TICKS

Ticks are another blood-sucking parasite that may be found on a dog. Ticks spend a few days feeding on the dog, gradually becoming distended. They drop off when fully engorged. It is a mistake simply to pull off a tick with tweezers without first cutting off its air-supply for about 30 minutes with a smear of grease. If not killed in this way, the head-part will remain firmly embedded in the dog's skin.

MANGE MITES

Demodectic mange may show mild symptoms of inflamed skin and hairless lesions or, more seriously, pustules and severe irritation. Prompt veterinary treatment is essential, as postponement may led to permanent baldness.

Sarcoptic mange is contagious to dogs and to man. It causes intense irritation and scabs on skin. Urgent veterinary treatment is needed, and isolation.

EAR MITES

Ear mites are responsible for ear mange, which causes great suffering and may lead to permanent ear damage. The dog shakes its head and carries it at a different angle. There may be a discharge and loss of balance. Most ear problems respond well to veterinary care.

WORMS

Many worms species can infest dogs and puppies. Some are transmissible to man, and can have particularly serious effects on children, including blindness. For this reason, dogs' faeces should be cleaned up, and dogs should be kept away from children's play areas. Children should also wash their hands after playing with dogs.

Puppies should be routinely treated against roundworm and adult dogs should be wormed regularly, in accordance with veterinary advice. This should also be sought promptly if a dog has tapeworms. Segments of tapeworm, which look rather like rice-grains, will probably be seen in its faeces.

RINGWORM

Ringworm is a highly contagious infection caused by a fungus rather than a worm. Round, bare, encrusted patches develop in a dog's coat. The infection can be quickly transmitted to people, and children should not touch an infected dog. Urgent veterinary treatment is essential.

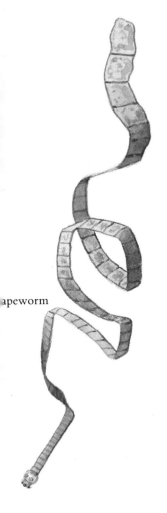

apeworm

Administering medicines

Liquid medicine This is administered with a helper holding the muzzle closed, and in a raised position. It is then possible to pour the liquid into a pouch of loose skin at the side of the mouth. Allow the dog time to swallow.

Tablets The method is to open the top jaw with one hand and the lower jaw with the other, leaving thumb and forefinger free to place the tablet well back on the tongue. Close the muzzle; stroke throat to assist swallowing.

Eye drops Again using a helper to hold the dog, unless it is very tractable and sure of you, apply the drops to the inner corner of the eye. If the head is in the raised position, the drops will run over the eyeball naturally.

Ear drops When needed, ear drops should be applied with a dropper. Hold the dog's head on one side, while they run into the ear canal.
  Take very great care when cleaning away discharge from the ears.

First aid

In an emergency, veterinary attention should be sought immediately. Do not rush an injured dog to the surgery but phone and ask for advice first.

   The aim of first aid is to ease pain and prevent injuries from becoming worse; in major emergencies it may save a dog's life. Learning first aid techniques is best done by example, and some training schools or local RSPCA inspectors will give instruction. But even without knowledge of these techniques there are several things which can be done to limit an animal's suffering. An injured dog will be frightened, and in all cases should be kept as quiet and comfortable as possible.

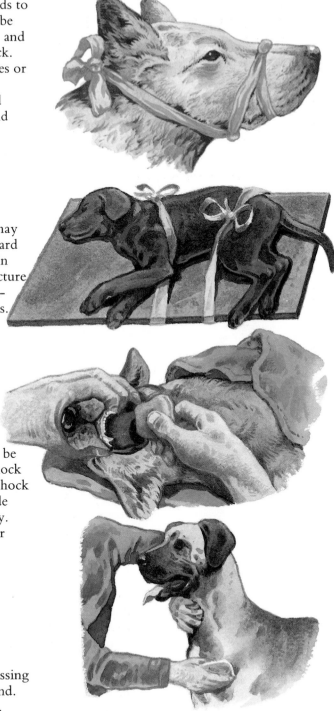

an injured dog is conscious, it needs to
 secured until veterinary help can be
ven. Approach calmly and gently, and
op an improvised lead over its neck.
nless the dog has breathing troubles or
aw injury, apply a tape muzzle,
oped over the muzzle then crossed
neath the chin and tied high behind
e ears.

oving an injured dog should be
oided if at all possible, but, for
stance after a road accident, this may
 necessary. Slide a door or flat board
der the dog then tie the casualty in
ace. In less severe cases where fracture
 not suspected, small and medium-
zed dogs can be carried in the arms.

urns and many other injuries may be
companied by shock. A dog in shock
eathes fast and has pale gums. If shock
 suspected, place the dog on its side
d (if unconscious), clear its airway.
over with a warm blanket or other
overing.

alt bleeding from a wound by pressing
pad of fabric firmly over the wound.
aintain pressure until help arrives.

Reproduction

VETERINARY CHECK-UP

If it is decided that a particular pair is to be used for breeding, both dog and bitch will need to have a veterinary check-up, prior to mating, to ensure there is no evidence of hereditary defects, infection of the genitalia or transmissible disease. The presence of a hereditary condition is a strong reason for having the dog or bitch neutered. Such defects could be passed on to the litter to the detriment of the individual puppies, as well as to the breed as a whole.

Parasitic problems such as skin mange, fleas, lice, or roundworm infestation can also be identified during a veterinary check-up, and the necessary treatment given. This is an important safeguard for the pups as well as for the sire and dam. This is also, of course, the time to check that the dam's vaccinations are up to date.

MATING

The best age to mate a bitch for the first time is during her second or third season, depending on the frequency of oestrus. She is receptive for a few days only, usually just after her bleeding stops, which is part-way through the second week (11–13 days). The dog should be a year old, or more. For mating, introduce the bitch to the dog in a safe enclosure at his home, or on neutral ground. They will need to be left together for some time, as copulation may take as long as 30 minutes. It is usual to introduce them on two consecutive days, to increase the chance of conception.

MISALLIANCE

Never try to separate a pair of copulating dogs while they are standing back to back, still 'tied'. If a bitch is discovered to have slipped out to a dog, and the alliance is unacceptable, a veterinary surgeon can give an injection to avoid pregnancy, providing the bitch is taken to him within 72 hours, and preferably within 24 hours. This has the effect of inhibiting the implantation of the fertilized eggs in the wall of the uterus so that conception is prevented, but the season is lengthened – perhaps by a further two weeks.

PSEUDO-PREGNANCY

After the period of oestrus, or heat, a bitch which has not been successfully mated may, nevertheless, develop all the physical and behavioural signs of pregnancy, and yet there will be no developing pups in the uterus. This rather disturbing condition, common in bitches, is known as pseudo, false, or phantom pregnancy. It tends to recur after each season and often leads to pyometra, which is a severe infection of the uterus. Spaying will prevent this condition occurring.

PREGNANCY

True pregnancy lasts 63 days, or nine weeks, within the range 55–66 days. It is not advisable to change the bitch's environment during this time, not only for the stress it would cause her, which could adversely affect the pregnancy, but also because her body would have insufficient time to re-adjust to the bacteria and viruses in a new place.

For the first month the bitch will need no special care, except that her abdomen should not be handled unduly. During the last four or five weeks of pregnancy the bitch, which may be carrying as many as six puppies if she is a small breed, or twelve if she is a large breed, will need to have her diet increased in quantity and quality. In particular, feed extra meat and milk and a vitamin/mineral supplement.

During the last fortnight of pregnancy, the bitch must be separated from other dogs, given newspapers and other materials, and encouraged to use the whelping bed prepared for her in a quiet place where she will have some privacy.

WHELPING

Up to the time of whelping, the bitch will be eating possibly three times her normal diet. When birth is imminent, within 24 hours probably, she will suddenly refuse all food, and her body temperature will drop to 37.8°C/100°F.

A few days before the bitch is due to whelp, it is prudent to arrange for her to have a veterinary examination. If there is likely to be any difficulty with the birth – for instance, because she has a small pelvis, and the puppies are likely to have wide heads (e.g. Chihuahuas) – the veterinary surgeon will say whether he should be called out.

Most bitches are capable of giving birth with no help, other than reassurance, from the owner. Exceptions are those which strain hard continuously for two hours without producing a pup: those which have no contractions; and those which show so little interest in the puppies that they do not even release them. In these circumstances, the veterinary surgeon should be consulted by telephone.

The puppies develop along the horns of the uterus, which is Y-shaped, and during labour are normally expelled first from one horn and then the other. Each puppy is born enveloped in a membranous sac and is released when the dam nips the sac. Each is followed by its own placenta or afterbirth, which the bitch may eat. Some veterinary surgeons recommend removal of the afterbirth, since it can cause a black diarrhoea in the bitch. It is necessary to check that the number of placentas equals the number of puppies, for a retained placenta may set up a uterine infection. Check, too, that no puppy's umbilicus is bleeding.

PUPPIES

The puppies are born at intervals of 30 minutes to 1 hour, which gives the dam some respite and time to clean, dry and stimulate each puppy before the next arrives. It may take just a few hours for a small litter to be completed: eight hours, or longer, for a large number of puppies.

The puppies need warmth and the dam's milk. The bitch 'noses' each puppy in turn towards a teat to suckle. This first milk, or colostrum, is essential. It has a high protein and vitamin content, acts as a natural purgative to expel the accumulated faeces, or meconium, from the puppy and, very importantly, contains antibodies which give early immunity from the infectious diseases.

A veterinary surgeon should be asked to check the puppies at about three weeks, by which time many will need worming. This early worming, in particular should be done on veterinary advice. Worming will only be effective if the correct dose is given, and repeated after an appropriate interval.

WEANING

Weaning is the gradual changeover from suckling the dam to independent feeding by the pup. As early as two weeks, especially when the dam has a large litter, it is wise to encourage the puppies to lick droplets of milk dabbed on to their noses with the fingertips. As soon as the puppy progresses from licking to lapping, small amounts of skimmed milk can be offered. At the same time, flakes of white fish and/or shredded boiled chicken can be given.

By the age of six weeks a puppy may be fully weaned and feeding on four meals a day: two of meat; and two of milk and cereal such as puppy meal, cooked rice, baby cereal and porridge. However, even if fully weaned, it is important for the puppy to stay with the dam for a further two weeks in order to become sturdier and to develop immunity against the normal bacteria in its environment. When the puppy goes to its new home, at eight weeks, it is then far less likely to contract diarrhoea and other digestive problems.

Dogs and the law

DOG REGISTRATION

Stray dogs cause many problems in the community – dog fouling, road accidents, and attacks on people and animals. The old licence was abolished in 1988 but the RSPCA believes that a compulsory national registration scheme with the permanent identification of dogs (through silicone chip implant or tattooing, in addition to the existing collar tag) must be introduced to encourage responsible ownership. The revenue raised from registration fees would go towards a network of dog wardens who would pick up stray dogs and attempt to reunite them with their owners and administer the law against irresponsible owners.

DOG COLLARS

It is compulsory for a dog to wear a collar, bearing the owner's name and address, when in a street or public place. This applies to all pet dogs, although certain others, such as packs of hounds and working sheepdogs, have exemption.

Identity disc, as required by law

DOGS AND NUISANCE

Local authorities in the UK have the power to designate certain roads in which dogs must not only wear a collar and identification, but must also be kept on a lead. There may also be bylaws which provide penalties for owners or keepers of dogs which foul public places or which, by repeated barking, cause a nuisance to local residents.

DANGEROUS DOGS

If a magistrates' court, upon complaint, considers that a dog is dangerous and not properly controlled, even if on the owner's property, it may make an order requiring the owner to control the dog, or alternatively it may order the dog to be destroyed and can appoint a person to carry out the destruction.

In addition, the owner may be disqualified from having custody of a dog for a certain period. Substantial penalities may be imposed for breach of such an order or for failure to hand over a dog for destruction.

DOGS WORRYING LIVESTOCK

The owner or person in charge of a dog found to be worrying livestock is likely to be prosecuted and also to be held liable for heavy damages. In Britain the dog may also be made the subject of a control or destruction order. (Livestock in this case means cattle, sheep, goats, pigs, horses, asses, mules and poultry.) A farmer who shoots a dog in these circumstances is legally in a strong position.

DOGS INVOLVED IN ACCIDENTS

Any driver involved in a road accident with a dog must stop. It is an offence to drive on, knowingly leaving the dog to suffer. The accident must be reported to the police.

The owner of a dog judged to have caused an accident may be liable to third party claims for damage. Readers are advised to buy suitable insurance cover against such a contingency.

SUSPECTED CRUELTY CASES

Any reader suspecting that a dog is being subjected to cruelty should ask the RSPCA to investigate the case in confidence. The Inspectors are contacted via the local Group Communciations Centre, which will be listed in the telephone directory under the Royal Society for the Prevention of Cruelty to Animals.

QUARANTINE REGULATIONS

Strictly enforced UK quarantine laws that require dogs, cats and many other mammals to spend six months in approved quarantine premises on entering the country from abroad have kept Britain virtually free of rabies for over fifty years, although the disease is endemic to most of the world.

Since rabies is now spreading across Europe towards the west, the present fear is that just one pet or stray dog, smuggled in illegally, without the precaution of quarantine, could introduce the disease.

The above is specific to the United Kingdom, but similar laws and regulations are in force in many other countries.

Your questions answered

How often should I bath my dog?

It used to be thought that bathing harmed a dog's coat, an
indeed it shouldn't be a weekly event. But a bath from tim
to time has benefits, and it may be the only way of cleanin
your dog if he has rolled in something smelly or stick
which will not brush out. There may be medical reason
too: your veterinary surgeon may prescribe bathing as pa
of a remedy for a skin infection, and several anti-fle
treatments come in the form of a shampoo.

Since bathing a dog – especially a large one – can be quit
a performance, it is usually better tackled by two peopl
Always use a shampoo specially formulated for dogs, an
be careful to rinse the coat thoroughly. The dog shoul
then be meticulously dried (with towels or a hairdryer) an
in winter, kept indoors for several hours afterwards.

My dog is a barker. The smallest thing sets him off, and it's upsetting the neighbours. How can I cure him?

A noisy dog is very difficult to live with, and your neig!
bours are within their rights to be upset. They could eve
take legal action against you, so the problem certainly nee
to be viewed seriously. First, examine your dog's lifestyl
Is he getting enough exercise? Or is he left alone for lon
periods, with nothing to do but watch (or listen to) passer
by? Dogs are social animals. If they are bored or lonel
they can easily develop habits like neurotic barkin
Changing your dog's daily routine may cure the problem
If not, you should enrol your dog and yourself on a
intensive training course without delay. Veterinary su
geons and local libraries have details of courses in your are

My dog has smelly breath. Would it help if I cleane his teeth?

You could certainly try – if he'll let you! Use warm wat
and a fairly soft toothbrush. As with human teeth, bru
downwards (or upwards) from gum to teeth, not acro

About once a week is enough. However, your dog's smelly breath may well be caused by a build-up of thick, hard tartar on his teeth. This can only be removed by a veterinary surgeon. Afterwards, supplement the tooth-brushing routine by giving your dog plenty of hard biscuits to chew.

My dog is afraid in the car. How can I help her?

For no apparent reason, some dogs are frightened by car travel. The cure lies in patience and persistence. Take the dog on frequent short trips ending in a treat (a walk, a game on the beach etc). Check that she is sitting in the place she finds most comfortable. To do this, let her choose her own position (within the limits of safety), and experiment by giving her a blanket or cushion as a comforter. Encourage and reassure her constantly, and *don't give up*; success can come very suddenly, just when it's least expected.

Should I keep my dog indoors on Fireworks Night?

You certainly should. Fireworks are terrifying to animals and you should not be tempted to let them off in your own garden if you have pets. If a roaming pet is startled by a firework, it might run so far from the source of its fear that it gets lost. On Fireworks Night, take your dog out for a walk before it gets dark. If it needs to go out briefly during the evening, keep it on the lead – even in the garden. If your dog is exceptionally frightened by fireworks, you should consult your vet in good time so that tranquillizers can be prescribed.

My middle-aged dog has suddenly become very bossy, growling and even nipping me. Why has this happened, and how do I regain control?

This is a problem that needs urgent action, before your dog's behaviour brings serious consequences. It is unusual for an adult dog's personality to change dramatically, but it could be that something has upset your pet deeply enough to bring out some latent personality trait. Some dogs – especially those bred for herding or guarding – are naturally assertive, and this quality can get out of hand if an owner does not retain his or her status of 'pack leader'. However, start by checking if the disturbance has a physical cause. Take your dog to the veterinary surgeon for a check-up and explain the problem to him. He may well be able to suggest strategies that will help you re-establish control. Ask, too, about dog training 'refresher courses'.

Life history

Scientific name	*Canis familiaris*
Gestation period	63 days (approx.)
Litter size	1–6 (small breeds) 5–12 (large breeds)
Birth weight	100 g/3½ oz– 500 g/1 lb 2 oz
Eyes open	10 days
Weaning age	35–49 days
Weaning weight	1000 g/2 lb 4 oz (small breeds)
Puberty	males 8–12 months females 6–18 months (commonly 8 months)
Adult weight	1000 g/2 lb 4 oz– 70 kg/150 lb
Best age to breed	males 350+ days females 540+ days
Oestrus (or season)	2 seasons per year
Duration of oestrus	3 weeks
Retire from breeding	males 8 years females 6–8 years
Life expectancy	10–18 years (small dogs usually outlive larger breeds)

Record card

record sheet for your own dog

(photograph or portrait)

Name

Date of birth
(actual or estimated)

Breed   Sex

Colour/description

Breeding notes

Medical record   Breeding record (if applicable)

Date of seasons for bitch

Date of neutering operation

Vaccinations

Veterinary surgeon's name   Surgery hours

Practice address

Tel. no.

Index